Palewell Press

TRAVELS OF A SPIDER

Camilla Reeve

Travels of a Spider

Printed and Bound in the United States
Published by Palewell Press, London, UK, 2006

First edition
Copyright ©2006 Camilla Reeve All Rights Reserved

Design and illustrations ©2006 Camilla Reeve

Cover image ©2006 Edward Feather
Contact: EdwardFeather@yahoo.com

ISBN: 978-0-95567-700-7

TRAVELS OF A SPIDER

This poetry collection is dedicated with love and thanks to my wonderful family, who are so supportive of my writing, and to each of my dear friends, you know who you are!

Camilla Reeve 2006

ACKNOWLEDGEMENTS

Poems from this collection have previously appeared in the Swanage Poetry Competition Anthology 1991, the Tears in the Fence Poetry Competition Anthology 1995, Ammonite 1995, the Ledbury Poetry Festival "Freedom Wall for Torture Victims" 2000 and the Salisbury Cathedral Holocaust Memorial Service Anthology 2001.

CONTENTS

Title poem – Travels of a spider   7

Part 1 - Dreaming of many journeys   9
The long journey of humans   9
Spring is sprung   11
Dreaming of you   12
London garden at night   13
Half past midnight   14

Part 2 – Extensions of herself   15
Life flows   15
The one thing   17
The kettle's song   18
Magic maker   20
Hero   21
Fistful   22
Quiet times   22

Part 3 - The limits of her world   23
The observatory   23
London's Eye   27
Unanswered   28
Harvest Moon, Deisel and Four Star   30
Unwitnessed   31
The Givens   32
Troubadour   34

Part 4 - Homes in other countries   35
House place   35
City at 6 a.m.   36
Pride in Steel   38
Last leg of a wise man's journey   40
Dark bird turning   42

Part 5 - Hillsides lost in snow   43
February snow   43
Near Oslo   44
Health Warning   45
Spider's web   45
Wild fire   46
River with no name, Cumbria   47
Other people's places   48

Part 6 - Hearts of the lonely   49
The Run-off   49
Children sent away   51
Death-mates at Khafji   52
Endland   54
Search party for a child   55
Some days just end in sadness   56

Part 7 - Centered once again   57
My last mountain   57
Mandela's freedom   58
Coming home via New York   60
Thoughts from Prison   62

Travels of a spider   02/07/1999

A spider builds her web,
going on many journeys
to the limits of her world
and anchoring with threads,
extensions of herself
so – centered once again –
disturbance near an anchor
sends messages to her

A poet charts her road,
dreaming of many journeys –
to homes in other countries,
to hillsides lost in snow,
to the hearts of the lonely –
letting down each anchor
woven out of words,
sticking to the strangeness
with her empathy.

1 ~ Dreaming of many journeys

The Long Journey of Humans   08/1997

How *old* was I last night ?
In the darkness and quiet
of my own back garden,
I looked up at a sky, deep indigo,
brushed with clouds of grey,
uplit apricot from the city,
and I felt so *young*.

/continued

The Long Journey of Humans (cont'd) 08/1997

The long journey of humans
stretched far ahead of me
full of promise and wonder.
The eyes of unnamed stars
peered down between the clouds
as strangers, hoped for friends,
glance from the corner of a rock
and make a new land homely.

Standing there, I heard nothing
but wind riffling my hair,
rain dripping from leaves,
the muffled stealth of paws
as a hunting cat passed by.

Now that the everyday,
with its crowded streets
and well-worn time-tables,
is round me, I might be feeling
as old as humanity and stale.
But I discovered in my mind,
and smiling, the little girl
who stood there in the dark.

She is still full of wonder
and delight, still looking out
and up and round her
at the enchanting and unknown,
where the return of daylight
has not this time achieved
the death of promise
or the end of mystery.

Spring is sprung! 27/01/2002

On Tuesday, when you said
that 'Spring is sprung!'
it had the sound of beds, upholstered, vast,
tried out by laughing newly-weds
in metropolitan department stores.

The floor detective's gaze
is brassy-bound,
it warns their hands away from zips and buttons
but more and more they long to mate
curled up on damask silk divans.

As steel springs make beds bouncy
for vernal equinoxes –
unbridled sex surrounded by sweet slumber –
Spring's coming sometimes is announced
by driving rain and gusty roar,

but a gentle ping just resounded
through the half-open window,
and, without great sounding brass, it whispered
into my mind's own optimistic ear,
'At last we've reached the turning of the year'.

Dreaming of you   **01/09/1998**

In last night's dreaming, you
still stood by the lagoon
but shadows masked your face.

Migrating swallows raced
across a dark sky bruised
by used up summer.

A sense of waiting,
of parched containment,
pressed down on that bare place.

Reeds thirsted for rain,
mouth burned for your kisses,
heedless, wind hissed around us.

It wasn't just a dream -
longing has undermined me.
I am no longer who you left behind.

London garden at night   16/10/1999

A windless night in autumn.
It's quiet enough
to hear a train
ten streets away,
or someone's bath
run down the drain,
and almost hear
a single snail
make silver trails
across the mossy flagstones.

Indoors, the last spin-cycle
flings washing round
our old machine,
and arguments
reach in at us
through TV screens,
but I'm out here
with open ears
and relishing
this near approach to silence.

Half past midnight   14/02/1986

Half past midnight,
where are you going to, my love,
my little one?
Half past midnight,
now you are going fast, but where
my darling one?

Half the time left,
out of our limited supply
has slipped away.
Half the time left
seems to have shrunk a bit in size
as you have done.

Time we should share
trickles away in sighs and tears
and wasted breath.
Time we should love
washes right past my grieving face
towards your death.

2 ~ Extensions of herself

Life Flows 13/09/1985

Each time I pause beside an autumn stream
and look across its restless, tumbled face
the water shows no definite design,
no certain pictures of what comes to me.
Leaves floating by betray a rusty gleam -
red-shifted from green shades into the dark
by the strong pulse of ever-passing days.
They should be warning me -
life flows, death comes, nothing goes on forever.

/continued

Life Flows (cont'd)   13/09/1985

But I can shed the image of dead leaves,
sweeping it simply from my present thoughts
and concentrate the whole of my attention
on berries ripening above the bank.

Still, when the river's full in early spring,
light welling up from it in every part,
piercing the wild silk grey of evening
with the repeating patterns of the stars,
shouldn't I grieve for our mortality,
the millions who have seen this sight before,
the many millions that are yet to live?
They are not born again,
life flows, death comes, nothing goes on forever.

Yet I accept the briefness of our stay here,
our struggles and confusions on the way,
Life's mystery in which we all take part,
each brushing Heaven's shoulders for a day.

Rather it's in the summer, when the rain
has faintly stirred the surface of a pool,
I seem to catch reflections of your face
bent down to hide the traces of your tears,
and I know absolutely as I stand there then,
however long it takes to span the years,
somewhere, some day, I'll stand beside your grave,
and I will mourn for you,
life flows, death comes, nothing goes on forever.

The one thing   01/03/1996

The year Mum died,
once I knew she was dying
and before she could do nothing
but lie there or be carried,
look at Dad or at the sky,
that's when she asked me,
'What would you really like?
What's the one thing
I could do for you
that you most want?'

And I said 'Stroke my head –
out of everything you did
from when I was a child,
that's what I most want now,
once more before you're dead.'
Gently she turned me round,
and laid me on the couch
as if it was a bed
then, hand across my head,
stroked me like a baby;
starting at the bridge of my nose,
drawing her palm, fingers together,
over my eyes to make them close,
over my forehead, soothing my fears,
over my hair, catching odd strands
on cracks that lined her hands,
hurting a bit, loosening my tears,
freeing me from the need
to beg her, 'Stay with me',
she'll always be with me.

Now it's *my* turn to ask,
my darling special daughter,
what's the one thing
I can do for you
that you most want?

The Kettle's Song   20/10/1998

While the cats wander
the kitchen feels too quiet.
I flick the kettle's switch
and stand quite still,
hands resting lightly
on its handle, white plastic,
the unlikely, wayward curve
of a young girl's arm in sleep.

Under my fingers
the kettle is vibrating,
starting to sing,
its muted rushing
like warm breezes
through lines of washing.
The steamy purr strengthens,
fills the emptiness.

I should be getting
toast and coffee ready,
making myself useful,
but I just stand there,
dream of drinking tea,
my mind elsewhere,
as the noise peaks
then gradually reduces.

/continued

The Kettle's Song (cont'd)   20/10/1998

Beyond the window,
the garden is still dark,
the cats still absent
prowling on strangers' roofs.
The spider-plant's pale limbs
stretch out so longingly
for someone, something,
whoever they belonged to.

And I miss you, so much,
miss you, miss you,
more than I thought it
possible to do.
Distractedly,
I flick the switch back on
and listen to the
kettle's lonely song.

Magic maker 27/08/1998

On the last day
she filled a sack
with all the shells
from Koukounaries,
and the white stone
found at Lalaria.
Then, with the stick
goatherds could use
that wouldn't fit
into her suitcase,
walked to the beach
to weave a spell.

There she arranged
the stone and shells
in a long snake,
walled up the sea
to stop it leaving
on the next plane.
The stick she placed
upright in sand
to herd the waves
in case they strayed
when she'd gone home
to England.

Hero   10/03/2005

I'm looking at you,
sitting right up close
and keeping really quiet
but all the time my mind
is saying 'Hero'.

I can't deny your prowess
in the courtrooms,
your courage in the war-zones
but the heroism
you demonstrate today
is even greater –

stray spurts of humour
in the face of fear,
singing comic songs
while taking cancer pills,
using your crutches
to 'row' your wheelchair
along the corridor
so you can give
love and support to Gill,

accepting with a grin
the sheer impossibility
of doing anything
with the finesse
your fingers used to have
but trying anyway;
this is rare courage,
my darling hero.

Fistful 06/1987

I have happiness
right here in my fist.
I hold happiness
as other women hold
hot dogs or cold cash.
And my happiness
is a close lay with you
and a fistful of your hair.

I know what it is
to go mad with dancing
late into the night
and in dark windows
to catch, glancing,
glimpses of my madness
and simply feel delight.
Happy fist, no history,
only this moment with you.

Quiet Times 30/03/1986

Quiet times
with your arms around me,
Quiet times
when we lie together,
and the scent of you,
warm and clean and true,
drifts across the stream
of my dreaming soul.
Quiet, quiet times.

3 ~ The limits of her world

The observatory 20/01/1995

Beside a road somewhere
from Edgware to Mill Hill
stands an observatory,
white painted, neat and still
from which are seen -
so scientists maintain -
stars at the reaches
of the universe.

In a street nearby
to the observatory
lives Pam, who has
a son, two daughters and
a job among the telescopes,
polishing the lenses.
Through them she peers
at light from long-dead stars

/continued

The observatory (cont'd) 20/01/1995

but she never sees
what passes close to home
inside her only son,
as he tries to understand
why five GCSEs, four
years of college, three
summers searching
don't guarantee a job,

why - to the Dole clerks -
young men like him are yobs.
Long haired, long minded,
seeing far into the future
yet seemingly unable
to conjure decent work
from petrol-laden air
between Mill Hill and Edgware.

Pam the cleaner's eyes
will pause sometimes,
eager to see novas
burst into distant life,
stars hurl themselves
towards oblivion
before they're even
named on stellar charts.

But she doesn't see
what bursting from the heart
of her first daughter,
who's hurling herself
towards anonymous
and probable death
on the cocktail of a wing,
a prayer and three white pills.

/continued

The observatory (cont'd)　　　20/01/1995

Still the observatory
searches the skies.
Its roofs open and shut
letting automatic eyes
suck in a cosmic vision
for anyone who cares
to scan the printout,
dots on a milky ground.

Pam polishes the printer,
lets her duster drift
across the paper.
The dots mean nothing to her
but the place she works
and so much paper wasted
every night she's tempted
to write a message on it:

'Eight bags of this stuff
is equal to one tree!'
But even Pam who,
after years, knows this,
is not prepared to see
the universe enfolded
in the mind of her third child
before it's shaped by school.

So when the girl is awe-struck
by the electric, spinning,
apple-dropping forces
of her native world,
Pam merely nods,
she's heard it all before.

/continued

The observatory (cont'd)   20/01/1995

The child's mind is
absorbing what it should.
Spontaneous creation
of knowledge this is not.
Knowledge is something
scientists have that fits them,
she believes, for well-paid jobs
behind the neatly painted
doors of an observatory.

It justifies employing her
to clean the workplace
in honour of the ones
who move there
and of the distant worlds
whose light they view there,
in casual disregard of
marvels close to home –

the lives and thoughts
of sons and daughters,
of parents and of trees,
which coexist so near
to the observatory
that, through its neutral,
distance-focused eyes,
they simply can't be seen.

London's Eye   08/2000

London's Eye above
and Thames below
see what they see,
keep secret what they know.

Four squat towers
rise from oily water,
moisture splashes down
out of choked-up gutters,
the whole sad structure
of Waterloo Bridge
lies in wait for us.
By pools of urine,
a dog sits with three men,
whose hats turned upside down
and upturned lives
reflect the town.

In a virtual world
I would build no bridges
that beggars had to sit on,
I would let no dogs
keep rough sleepers with them,
I would hear no music
that must played on whistles
by men without a home.
Only, who wants a world
without a bridge, a dog, a tune,
we need to sort out this one,
but until then . . .

London's Eye above
and Thames below
see what they see,
keep secret what they know.

Unanswered 24/11/2000

bus stations are full of noises
that cannot be explained
and rules to be obeyed:

'Bus drivers must switch off
their engines while on stand'
'Max headroom four metres'
'Don't give coins to beggars
or bird-seed to pigeons -
it will simply encourage them'.

waiting for my bus, I miss you,
a phone rings four times
somewhere out of sight
in one of those rooms
where light still shines
on empty, ash-burned lino,
four times then falling silent

who was it stood or sat
at the other end of the line,
tapping their fingers,
rubbing sleepless eyes,
begging you in their mind
to just pick up the phone,
what was it that they wanted?

/continued

Unanswered (cont'd)   24/11/2000

love itself is full of rules:-
lovers must guess who's calling
before they see the number;
or know you couldn't call
and not reproach you;
if they truly loved you
they would understand
why you still call and call
when nothing's left to say

as we pull away
the phone starts up again,
shrilling unanswered,
filling me with questions

Harvest Moon, Diesel and Four Star   10/2000

Crackle of ice underfoot on the forecourt,
rustle of cellophane ripped from fag packets,
optical shock as a Harvest Moon pops
into our sight next to Diesel and Four Star.

I say 'Parish Lantern!' and see my friends nodding,
in a month full of moons this takes the first prize
though none of us know just what parish we live in
or how to re-light a blown out storm lantern.

Our parents would gather soft fruit on long evenings,
we used it to linger far longer with lovers,
but our children will harvest great ropes of tomatoes
from cool hydroponics by light of Old Earth.

Unwitnessed   1991

Among the slowest hours of the night
when ribbons of time hang loose
and do not pull us clearly
from the last event towards the next,

lights blink but without haste,
their orange eyes as stealthy
and as sharp as hunting cats
upon the empty crossing that awaits.

A car sits waiting engine half undone
and steam is rising sluggishly
while out of sight and very faint,
from near the taxi-rank, two voices come.

A noise as if an engine had backfired
intrudes itself unwanted on my ears,
almost unwitnessed, but closely followed by
two men running, as slow as dreamers

who know themselves to be pursued
by vengeful demons. Just two men
running and a third, perhaps, behind
watching the gradual exit of his blood

and then no sound, no sign of life except
the crazy orange lights that keep on blinking
and seem to swear they really nothing saw
within this night that's dying from neglect.

The Givens   01/03/1998

Well you live where you live
(that's a given)
and you get the work you get
not some other.
The difference is vital,
if you're covering the rent,
meeting the credit payments,
you survive.

To get to work you travel
and your journey is a pain
or it's okay
but whichever way you go
by the train or car or bus
there are days when every choice
turns out slow.

Your home stands where it does
with the cars that are driven
past your door
by the other people who
also live where they live
and can't get to their work by
bus or tube.

All the cars make some noise
(that's a given),
a combination of their age
and how they're driven,
plus they also give off fumes
if they don't use special fuel
which the drivers would afford
if they could.

/continued

The Givens (cont'd)   01/03/1998

So the cars make noise and fumes
and your children either do
or don't get sick,
deafness, stress, pneumonia,
asthma, bronchitis, cancer,
when they're ill the doctors visit
or they don't.

The surgery or the hospital can
be walked or driven or bussed to
if there's time.
With their luck and pain and sweat,
with your love and fear and effort,
your children will get better
or they won't.
These are the givens.

Troubadour   31/01/2006

He makes haunting music
in the cut-through by the station,
notes that reach me
before I even see him,
chords of beauty.

He brings morning with him
to that shadowed stretch of tunnel;
sun on rooftops;
see my love tomorrow;
tumbling waters.

Stripped down and threadbare,
if his music sometimes stumbles,
hesitates, falters,
it make me wait for each anticipated chord,
as desperate and desiring as the
life he's forced to.

4 ~ Homes in other countries

House-Place   **12/05/89**

In the middle of the day,
in the middle of the village,
of the group of villages;
in the middle of a country edged by war;
in the middle of a continent
stands a round mud hut.

At the end of the path from the well,
at the end of the track from the road,
at the end of the walk from Sudan,
at the end of years of struggle for her beliefs,
and of being driven out and away
someone has made a home.

And written around its walls
in letters of blood and ash,
in letters of fear conquered,
in letters one hand wide are these words:
Man ot pa Regina -
This is Regina's hut.

City at 6 a.m.   04/01/1996

The city opens them at dawn,
its giant metal jaws,
greedy for a tasty tithe
of everybody's labour,
their sweat and hopes and lives.

Rhythmic, staccato, thumping chant,
section of track with two trains passing,
all lights illuminated,
one train enters the station
and one moves out of sight.

Full train seen through station window,
bright as cross-sections of a live volcano.
Purposeful bustling erupts,
these are business travellers
going somewhere they have rights.

Along the city streets,
in shop and office doorways,
hiding as far as possible
from weather and police raids,
migrant workers end their night.

Passing by them, dances of cars
play follow-my-leader,
big headlights disclosing
metre on cobbled metre
of carefully woven stripes.

/continued

City at 6 a.m. (cont'd)   04/01/1996

Snow-blown concentric circles
form heart-shapes with canals,
which over history drained,
from many hinterlands,
the city's early life –

Long barges filled with corn,
iron bars, timber and stone,
old tributes taken and gone –
The city swallows people now
far more than metal pipes.

On the canal, red and white
puddled lights radiate,
bridges frame them.
Swallowing people is no accident,
not in this vista thought out
for the burger-masters'
personal delight.

Pride In Steel   26/01/1990

I love to go where quarrying stone
has pared a hillside to the bone
and trace the ammonite's curled wave
while sunbeams spark on mica flakes,
where all is ours to name and take
and, with our craft, new products make
to grace the table, span the gorge
or find another use for forged
iron bars and tempered steel.

When Valparaiso stirs at dawn,
a harsh-voiced siren calls them in
from shanty town or lonely grove,
worn tools in hand, bent under loads,
thronging the gates on the steelyard road,
these are the men of steel.

As sun begins to flood the bay
showing the stress of yesterday,
- the empty faces lined with toil,
the wits that alcohol has spoiled,
the men with shirts already soiled –
have you no pride in steel?

Si, I have pride in steel, Señor.
I love to see new buildings soar
all bright and stark against the green
of hillsides forested and clean,
to know that future towns will rise
and thrust gray towers to the sky
making us seem, in foreign eyes,
both technical and wise -
it's only the costs I hate.

                                /continued

Pride In Steel (cont'd) 26/01/1990

I do have pride in making steel,
but you should live with us awhile
and tend the farms that miss their men
or wince as barefoot children run
through broken glass and open drains
where flowers are seldom seen.

Yet watching as the slip-way clears
to launch a ship that took two years,
so many hours of patient skill,
of bending metal to their will
and even working men she's killed
to reach the present day,

I must confess a common dream
with other members of this team
that drew the ship and laid their plans
and noted how the stresses ran,
that sweated in the puddle's glare
and washed the swarf from graying hair
with straining arms and backs that ache,
(and all for some ship-owner's sake
who has no pride in steel).

Where cranes are raised to frame the day
and goods have reached the holding bay,
respect is due to men whose skill
can shift a load with zero spills,
can sort a heap and speed a batch
and keep their cool when levers catch,
working them loose again.
Yes, I have pride in steel, but then
a greater pride in the men!

Last leg of a Wise Man's journey   24/12/2001

I saw him coming a long way off
turning his camel's head into the last straight
of the desert road before it rises up,
braced on rocky foundations, to meet the bridge.

The other two were already half-across,
their rich jewels and many coloured robes
glinted in the early sun of a day
that later would become the hinge of history.

He cannot have known I watched him
but he placed one hand across his eyes,
maybe it was to hide the sight
of burning truth blocking the road ahead.

And I, not knowing what would soon happen,
wondered why someone rich and powerful
hung back, as a boy behind his friends,
what could be daunting to a man like that?

Did he fear the loss of certainties
that shaped the world he grew in –
inherited beliefs or muttered incantations
against the evil eye and heathen men?

Or did he sense that now he stood alone,
as all of us must do in these dread times,
facing new wisdom that was even then
striving to be born in the back room of an inn?

/continued

Last leg of a Wise Man's journey (cont'd)

It's hard when someone first discovers
how closely all the world is linked,
neighbour to neighbour, brother to brother,
oneself to ones own worst enemy.

I saw him dig his heels into the camel
so it, inexorably, began to cross the bridge.
Above me, the city's towers blazed brighter in the sun
reflecting what was thundering to meet them.

Dark Bird Turning 11/2001

What news flies
on the wings of a dark bird,
midnight blue,
over a stranger's roof?
No news, brother,
except the tale you've heard
within your secret heart
when friend or child were late.

What luck hangs
from the claws of a vulture seen
turning and turning
over a foreign town?
No luck, sister,
except the kind we're born with
and joke about as children,
which now is wearing thin.

No news brother,
but my pain at your suffering,
no luck sister
but my prayer that we both survive.

5 ~ Hillsides lost in snow

February Snow   02/03/2004

February snow
lies longer in the woods
where a steep bowl
of caved-in tree roots,
all overgrown
with moss and bluebells,
conceals it from the sun.

On looking back,
through over-arching sprays
of sycamore and ash,
past far too many days
not visiting the woods,
the snowy patch,
though bright, is far away

yet never quite invisible.
It offers light
as long-imploded stars
still glimmer in the sky.

Near Oslo   17/12/1994

As the wind blows
and the shutters rattle
she begins to know
what it is that matters,
not why she has *come*
or what she must *do*
but that this place is
as she'd thought of it,

with its banked snow
blanketing from cold
gnarls of tree root
free to spread themselves,
dark between the trunks
where her glance can rest,
pale sky meeting branch
far as eye can reach,

so this whole land
is a living web
into which she sinks
with a surge of hope
that the world is
how she'd thought of it
and this place is
somewhere she can live.

Health Warning 01/08/2000

The pharmacist warned you it was
definitely the season
for hay-fever, and getting burrs on your jumper
from lying down in the cornfield
with your lover, and sneezing.

Spider's Web 12/09/1999

Few things are more
circular, astonishing, determinate,
insubstantial, effective, mysterious
than a spider's web.
Few things are more.

## Wild Fire			17/05/1998

You know
how bluebells used to show –
ravishing, unexpected,
misty-blue flickerings
over brown, under green –
the wood-ground's burning off
from many thousand
bunsens in the moss
of the Spring's first crazy
rush of gaseous life?

But now
there is a web-page
listing all the places
bluebells can be gazed at,
risk-free tourism today!
Hailstones not intervening
you could view them all.
Bluebells *would* be seen,
predictable, convenient,
an Internet event.

I won't be visiting that web-page
I'd rather take my chances with the Spring.

River with no name, Cumbria   21/06/1999

I wanted to write the sounds
but the words wouldn't do it,
down the hidden valley
waters made music.

I wanted to catch the rhythm
but I'm no musician,
just linking words didn't ease my
frustration.

In the hidden valley
waterfalls drumming,
pounding and gurgling,
air humming,

running through trees,
rivulets burbling,
looping and streaming,
sweet purring.

I wanted to sound the notes
but my words didn't show it.
River with no name
down the hidden valley
echoes in secret
inside my memory,
sending harmonics
but only to me.

Other people's places   02/02/2001

A scatter of crows
peck yellow grass
in half-arched,
bare-boughed
apple shade.

Serried larches
form wind-breaks
punctuated
by one dark yew
at twenty paces.

Other people's
lived-in places
that they've stared at,
paid for dearly,
loved to pieces.

One house vacant,
glassless windows
where the wind-sent
question lingers -
what is constant?

All that linked
yew, house and crow,
once known by those
who loved this land,
can make me think
of what needs mending
nearer home.

6 ~ Hearts of the lonely

The Run-Off   10/1994

He stood and stared at the run-off
for longer than his life, it seemed,
while the boom of the surf
hammered him into a waking dream
where only he existed
of all the billions in the world.

A thin boy staring at the run-off
as the tide's lick tore into the earth,
washing black wave against grey stone,
stealing slowly for its own reasons.

His body wished to run away,
in sweats and trembling it prepared,
not from the raging of the surf
which had a fascination,

                               /continued

The Run-Off (cont'd) 10/1994

the tearing of each stone fragment
from its mother or father rock,
accomplished with ruthlessness
but never malice or betrayal.

The sea does what the sea can
and then it waits, in restless
undulation with the land,
but people do, or promise to do
more than they should,
ask more than they're entitled to.

He stood and stared at the run-off,
watching the water and stone fragments
rush out on the sea's shoulders,
dreaming a path for them to other shores.

The sweats and trembling lessened;
step by step by step he went
to the edge of the earth he knew
and there he waited, a young fragment,

for the lick of the tide and
the boom of the surf to carry him
to a place where sleep was sound
and he'd never need to watch the sea again.

Children sent away   03/05/2001

the thrown stone has no say
in whether it comes back,
it didn't run to the station
and buy a one-way ticket
or lift a brick wall up
and beat its bones against it,
it just lay where it was chucked,
pity the thrown stone
and children sent away.

the spat drink has no right
to slip back in your mouth.
you spit children, they stay spat,
a stain across the carpet
or worse still, they learn spitting
and never can stay put,
sleeping on streets, faces shut,
pity the spat drink
and children sent away.

the next stone, make sure you write
your name and number on it
and write, also, the real reason
you're chucking it away
but if you run out of space
because the stone's too small
then put off throwing it
until another day
and wake up, stone thrower,
before it gets too late.

Death-mates at Khafji   31/1/91

These are the bodies, Sir,
you asked to view.

Side by side they stretch
across the sand as lovers,
one with his hand
upon the others,
faces turned each to each
and yet, not a new
Romeo and Juliet
but two young men.

The left one died
to take some land
that wasn't his,
to help some people
he had never met,
part of a war
defined as being just,
for country, God and peace.

His death-mate died
to hold some land
that wasn't his,
to hurt some people
who had hurt his friends,
for God and country
yet so much wishing
to fly home again in peace.

/continued

Death-mates at Khafji (cont'd)   31/1/91

They could be kin, skin dark,
hair curled as twins,
one seems to smile
and one died shouting.
I mourn the lack
of who they might have been.
Only respect -
I have to grant them that.

Their weapons gone,
the various shades of cloth
are all that show
which side they fought for.
Grey, fawn and brown,
meant to blend in with rock,
were not enough
to keep them safe that day.

There is no camouflage
when morning comes.
Stark light picks out
the labels on right feet,
the numbers in a log,
waiting for body bags
one black, one red,
to carry them away.

They might be brothers
maybe even friends.
Perhaps, some day,
their sons will be.
For these two here,
mated in death,
whatever I may dream,
their day is spent.

Endland   12/03/1998

Endland
He scratched the word into the thin partition
above the bin where pencil shavings fall
twisted as secrets whispered sharpening.

Suited him
to mock the name used for his foster nation,
the word he made was sour as lemon-juice,
as hard to eat as meat without an onion.

The sound
slid quick off tongue, short as his change when out,
a stunted word to mutter at the teacher
whose only way of speaking was a shout.

Penknife
he used to carve the letters wasn't his one,
they made him leave that when they ran away.
This country wouldn't ever be *his* one.

A boy
from somewhere jigsaw-bright at midday
trapped in a place that never changed from grey
feeling that chalk was eating up his brain.

Endland,
the end of hope, badger in blocked up hole.
He wrote about the grey mist choking him.
He scowled and muttered. No-one saw a thing.

Search-party for a child 15/01/1990

The shiver of the night is grey
around the shadows of a house.
Slowly raindrops fall.
Dust rises
from an empty hall
I wonder,
was he here at all?

How long a single night can seem
searching as in an waking dream,
having to be here,
nothing I achieve
frees me of my fear,
nowhere I believe
will I find my dear.

But searching has become my life,
probing, like a jealous wife;
how did he look?
was it long ago?
you knew him well?
Sorry, I have to know
to feed my private hell.

The shiver of this night is grey
around the shadows of this house.
Grief is a mother
shaking in the rain
after another
wasted evening's pain,
hadn't a chance of
finding him again,
not this time.

Some days just end in sadness   21/03/1998

When you walk, as I do,
on hardfaced city streets,
thrust yourself barenecked
through the heaviness of summer,
see boys and girls stretched out,
sleeping on those streets,
see some of them not sleeping
for fear of other people,
then your throat fills up
with useless unshed tears
and your heart implodes
on wishes unfulfilled.

So you turn for home
whether flat or house
with a lock to keep
you in and strangers out.
Safe home. Stupid home!
Not doing enough for others home!
Only, what can you do
but what you already did,
which never is enough?
And there is no doubt about it,
absolutely none, for I have tested
this proposition to destruction,

some days just end in sadness.

7 ~ Centred once again

My last mountain 21/01/1999

Call it

spiritual,
if you will

but my heart
had seen clouds part
like Turner's art

before my mind
had made the time
to do a climb
and get where I'm

expected.

Day's end comes
when the sun,
its full course run,

greets the mist
with a kiss

and sets.

Mandela's Freedom   10/02/1990

Freedom comes in the morning,
so they tell me, I hear it on
the broadcasts, the soldiers whisper -
white officer, black orderly together
whisper - new habits forming.

So it is coming, this time, I believe,
the freedom of which all speak
attributing it to me.
But what is this experience,
how will it differ from today's?
I am a free man in my heart
and have been so for years,

that is the secret of my strength.
In spite of my wife's tears
in spite of certain longings
to see my hills again, to walk
chest-high through seeding grasses
and bow my head only so wind
won't bring the water to
my eyes as swift it passes,
I have been free.

I spoke as no-one's servant
except our Saviour's.
I lived and breathed and thought
far from the Police,
far from the pressures of the crowd,
and in the heat-shimmering
silence of my cell at noon

/continued

Mandela's Freedom (cont'd)   10/02/1990

I spoke my thoughts aloud
with no authority to shut my mouth,
no state or followers
or Press to mark my words,
or mock and hunt me down
as they may do tomorrow.

Into the past I see myself
retreating, the self I have
preserved against adversity
and death of friends and
loneliness and untold sorrow,
that self could soon be gone.

Coming home via New York   21/06/1997

Last week you stood in Times Square,
once called The Heart of the World,
not by me or you even
but it beats at every hour
of day and night with the feet
and strident voices of people.

Their work, pleasures, energy are
jerky, abrupt, exciting.
You say it is much larger
than Piccadilly. Giant signs,
towers barnacled with light,
scintillations of brightness
struck your eyes, filling the painter
in you with surprised delight,
exhausting other senses.

Then you walked further on
to Greenwich Village, which you liked
but that too was larger
than you'd once imagined.
When you asked if it had grown
since Hemingway's time,
passers-by said 'No,
it's always been this size.'

/continued

Coming home via New York (cont'd) 21/06/1997

With everything so much larger,
brighter, than we have at home
a traveller might be forgiven
for finally believing New York
to be the Heart, but you didn't.
Instead, the morning after,
you carried on your journey
till you came to us at last.

To me, the Heart of the World
is when we are together,
you and I and the others,
in my mind or on the phone
or with my arms around you,
taller than I remember,
harder to hug the whole of,
I'm sure you must have grown,
every new inch as special.

Yet, your excitement at New York,
although it cannot make that city
the heart of my life or of yours,
made it more real and visible
from where we live, than songs
or even films have done before.

Thoughts From Prison   18/07/1986

I dream a day the sun will rise so high
that even we shall see it here and know
that bands of shadow match each band of light
so different from the neon's source-less glow.
Some morning on the fringes of my sleep
new gold will strike the wall above my head
and squinting I shall watch the dust-motes leap
and feel like springing swiftly from my bed.
I'll stand beside a window clear of bars
and see the mountains merging with the sky
and sense, however far away you are,
the sun is bringing tears to your eyes.

I smell the bread that you have yet to bake,
its fragrance rises through the silent gloom
disturbing sleepers yearning for a feast
their faces chalky and their arms too thin.
The kitchen table, lightly floured and bare,
shows where you'll stand the day that I come home,
smidgens of flour clinging to your hair
and shaking hands upon the rolling pin.
I feel your oven in the wave of heat
that strikes me as I cross the prison yard,
its door swings wide as you remove our bread,
the yeast of freedom rises in my heart.

                               /continued

Thoughts From Prison (cont'd)   18/07/1986

I hear the songs the children dare not sing,
the ones that make street corners seem too still,
no later rhythm can replace that lilt,
their voices sailed to Heaven on the breeze.
How many hours I listened in the square
while balls were thrown against the coolest wall
in time to words that came down centuries,
not understood but echoing with peace.
Old music from the throats of those I love
will one day burst, as rivers after rain,
I feel a tide of joy rise up in me
to hear the children's voices free again.

I keep my country in my deepest self,
in memories of childhood lit by love,
of sitting idly by a dusty road
untouched by thoughts of who might go and come.
I lean my back against a wooden fence
around a field my family have farmed
so long their names have overflowed the page
kept in the Bible by the oldest son.
I dream a country that is not here yet
whose streets are washed by rain and not by blood,
whose hills resound at dawn to mating birds,
whose people have both dignity and food,
a country where we all could live as one.

www.ingramcontent.com/pod-product-compliance
Lightning Source LLC
Chambersburg PA
CBHW020022050426
42450CB00005B/606